*To my brothers and sisters,
some of whom have moved to
other cities, but all of whom
love Richmond.*

Old photographs used in Richmond Illustrated *were acquired, in part, through a grant from the John Stewart Bryan Memorial Foundation, Inc.*

Published by The Dietz Press
109 E. Cary St., Richmond, VA 23219

Typesetting by PAGE, Inc., Richmond, VA

Library of Congress Card No., L. C. 93-090392

RICHMOND ILLUSTRATED

Unusual Stories of a City

Written and Illustrated by David D. Ryan

Contents

"Citys in the Air" 14

"The house is on fire" 22

"At last we were off" 28

"Quarreling with the maggots" 36

Bizarre story 46

Thomas Jefferson's Capitol 52

Both men fired 62

Monument Avenue 66

The roof gave way 72

First woman bank president 76

The woman vanished 80

Richmond is shown in a 1796 painting by Benjamin Latrobe.

Richmond as it looks today in a view taken from the site of Rocketts Landing.

The Richmond-Petersburg Railroad Bridge, shown in this 1871 Harry Finn painting, burned in 1865 and 1882.

Richmond as it looks today from a similar view to Finn's painting. The Manchester Bridge is at left.

St. John's (Episcopal) Church as it looked in Patrick Henry's time.

St. John's Church today.

"Citys in the Air"

THE Powhatan Indians paused to watch the bald eagle circling above the forest-lined river. The majestic bird swooped down to the bubbling waters and clasped in its talons a black- and white-striped fish; the eagle's broad wings cupped the air and lifted the bird across the rapids and up to the top of a pine tree.

The Indians went back to spearing fish which charged up the dancing waters of this river they called "Powhatan." In the spring the water turned white with shad. The river also teemed with one hundred-pound sturgeon, and sometimes the Indians rode these fish for fun. Clams and mussels clung to the bottom of the river's boulders and rocks.

The river later would be named the "James" by other men, who this very day, May 23, 1607, were exploring it in a shallop. Their skin was white; their faces were surrounded by

Indians found fish plentiful in the river they called "Powhatan."

beards, curling hair and broad-rimmed hats. They wore doublets and hose, and their leader was a one-armed soldier. They brought their boat to the north shore down river from the rapids and crossed a "playne" where grew "wheate, beane, peaze, tobacco" and "gordes." At the end of the plain they climbed a small hill where the roar of the river could be heard at fifteen log and mud buildings composing the village of Chief Powhatan.

The Indian chief "and some of his people satt" with the English explorers and ate "very freshly of our meat" and "dranck of our beere ...." Later the explorers' leader, Captain Christopher Newport, ordered his men back to the shallop to further explore the river, but their progress was impeded after a mile by the boiling waters of The Falls. The explorers stopped at a round island and there they knelt, prayed and erected a wooden cross with the inscription "Jacob Rex, 1607." Some of the Indians who accompanied them became upset at the strange ceremony, fearing the white men were stealing their land.

Over the next fifty years the English would establish a settlement and fort at The Falls; abandon them after an attack by the Iroquois Indians, and then return to establish profitable trade with the local Indians and those living west of the river.

One of the most successful traders was Thomas Stegg, Jr., who began acquiring land in 1659 and soon had on the south bank of the James River 1,800 acres he called "The Falls

Plantation." He died childless in 1671 and left his holdings to his nephew, William Byrd.

Byrd's first son, William II, was born at the plantation in 1674 and became heir to the land in 1704. William II, spent most of his early years studying in England, and it was 1726 before he gave up his frequent trips back there and settled down.

William Byrd II

During one of his inspections of his inheritance, he noted that the view from the hills overlooking the James River reminded him of the view of the Thames River at Richmond, England.

His interest in Virginia centered around plantation life at first — he built the great plantation at Westover between The Falls and Jamestown — and for several years he resisted using his land for a town. But in 1733 he made this entry in his notebook, *A Journey to the Land of Eden*:

> When we got home we laid the foundations of two large Citys. One at Shacco's, to be called Richmond, and the other at the point of the Appamattux River to be called Petersburg. These Major Mayo offered to lay out into lots without Fee or Reward. The truth of it is, these

> two places being the uppermost landing of [the] James and Apparnattux Rivers, are naturally intended for marts, where the Traffick of the Outer Inhabitants must Center. Thus we did not build Castles only, but also Citys in the Air.

Major William Mayo laid off for Byrd in 1737 a town of thirty-two squares covering an area from the crest of the present day Church Hill down to the river and back north to the crest of Shockoe Hill, now known as Capitol Hill. Byrd donated plots 97 and 98 for "The Church." St. John's Church was erected there in 1741, replacing "The Falls Chapel" built in 1717. There were two taverns already in operation when Mayo drew his plans, along with warehouses and Byrd's trading store. Byrd advertised in the *Virginia Gazette*, offering lots for "seven pounds in Virginia currency," on the condition that the buyer build a house within three years. In 1742 the Virginia Assembly passed legislation incorporating Richmond.

One of the first residents of the new city was Jacob Ege. He purchased land on lower Main street, and about 1739 built a small house with stone from the river. It is now known as the Old Stone House and is the home of the Edgar Allan Poe Museum.

Since its founding 260 years ago, Richmond has grown from a trading post to a major Southeast United States capital with a metropolitan population approaching three quarters of

The Ege women, members of Richmond's "first" family.

a million people. The years have brought tragedy and drama — American traitor Benedict Arnold burned the city in 1781. Richmond was the center for the Confederacy during the four years of America's deadliest war that ended with the city burning again. It was nearly one hundred years later before black citizens would be given their right to be equal. Famous visitors included the Marquis de Lafayette in 1781 and President Abraham Lincoln on April 4, 1865 after the city fell to the Union Army. British Prime Minister Winston Churchill visited the city in 1946, staying at the Governor's mansion and addressing a joint General Assembly.

Post Civil War Richmond saw a vigorous rebuilding led by such men as Lewis Ginter, Joseph Bryan, James H. Dooley, Joseph R. Anderson, James Thomas, Jr., Peter Mayo, Alexander Cameron, James B. Pace, Joseph G. Dill, Dr. R.A. Patterson, T.C. Williams, William R. Trigg, James Stewart, John P. Branch, Frederic R. Scott and others. At the turn of the century, Richmond was a major railroad center, and business and industrial successes built upon each other, slowing down only for recessions and the Great Depression. Even during times of downturn, the city has fared better than most.

In 1952 the late Floyd D. Gottwald shocked the industrial world when as president of Albemarle Paper Company, he borrowed $200,000,000 and bought Ethyl Corporation, eighteen times Albemarle's size — a "Jonah swallowed the whale" story. Besides Ethyl, other Fortune 500 companies are headquartered in metropolitan Richmond including Reynolds Metals Company, James River Corporation, Chesapeake Corporation, E.R. Carpenter, Universal Corporation, Specialty Coatings International, Inc., Crestar Bank, Signet Bank, Dominion Resources, Central Fidelity Bank, Life Insurance Company of Virginia and Circuit City.

In my 30 years of writing about Richmond and Virginia history, I am often asked to recount old stories about the city. On the following pages are some of my favorites, including original accounts of the Richmond Theater Fire in 1811, a trip on a canal boat along the James River and Kanawha Canal in the 1830's, the building of Thomas Jefferson's Capitol and the tragic courtoom collapse in that building in 1870, and the triangle love affair of Page McCarty, John B. Mordecai and Mary Triplett. I have also included many of my favorite old photographs and paintings, along with ones I have taken of similar scenes, contrasting the architecture that gives one the feeling of a city where the old and the new mingle to breathe the future.

David D. Ryan

"The house is on fire"

FOLLOWING the Revolutionary War and Benedict Arnold's raid, Richmond rebuilt and its citizens began enjoying a 28-year run of successful theater that began production in 1784 and ended in tragedy December 26, 1811.

That last night about six hundred fifty persons, 15 per cent of the town's population, crowded the recently built, three-story Richmond Theater on Shockoe Hill (now referred to as Capitol Hill). The audience included Governor George W. Smith and U.S. Senator Abraham B. Venable. The main play, "The Father," by Frenchman Denis Diderot had been completed and the audience was waiting for the second act of the after piece, "Raymond and Agnes of the Bleeding Nun." A shift in scenery involved the removal of a chandelier with a still burning candle. The property man ordered the chandelier lowered and in the confusion, the cords became entangled.

Patrons flee raging fire at the Richmond Theater.

The stagehand jerked the cords; the chandelier tilted and the scenery caught fire.

Thomas Ritchie, editor and publisher of the *Richmond Enquirer* told what happened next under the headline,

> **OVERWHELMING CALAMITY**:
>
> In the whole course of our existence, we have never taken our pen under a deeper gloom than we feel at this moment.... A whole theatre wrapt in flames — a gay and animated assembly suddenly thrown on the very verge of the grave — many of them, oh! how many, precipitated in a moment into eternity — youth; and beauty, and old age and genius overwhelmed in one promiscuous ruin — Shrieks, groans and human agony in every shape — this is the heart-rending scene that we are called upon to describe....
>
> Mr. (Hopkins) Robertson came out in unutterable distress, waved his hand to the ceiling, and uttered those appalling words — "The house is on fire,"... the cry of *fire, fire*, passed with electric velocity through the house — every one flew from their seats to gain the lobbies and stairs.
>
> The most heart-piercing cries pervaded the house. "Save me, save me." Wives asking for

Gilbert Hunt saved a dozen women.

> their husbands, females and children shrieking while the gathering element came rolling on its curling flames and columns of smoke — threatening to devour every human being in the building. Many leaped from the windows of the first story, and were saved — children and females of all descriptions were seen to precipitate themselves on the ground below — most of these escaped; though several of them with broken legs, and thighs, and hideous contusions.... But those in the boxes, above and below, pushed for the lobbies..., but so great was the pressure that they retarded each other; until the devouring element approached to sweep them into eternity....
>
> Oh miserable night of unutterable woe!

Governor Smith, Senator Venable and 75 others perished in the flames or died of injuries. Among the heroes was a black man, Gilbert Hunt, who stood under a window and caught about a dozen women as they were handed down to him. Monumental Church now sits on the site of the theater as a memorial, and ashes from those who died are encased in an urn there in the 1200 block of East Broad Street.

Monumental Church is a memorial to the 77 people who died in the Richmond Theater fire.

"At last we were off"

ONE of the visions George Washington had for developing America was a system to carry commerce from the Atlantic Ocean westward beyond the Allegheny Mountains, connecting up with the Ohio River. He envisioned ships carrying goods to the falls of the James River at Richmond and from there by packet boats through a system of canals and the river. He journeyed to Richmond in November 1784 to promote the idea and soon the James River Company was formed with Washington as honorary president. By 1786 the corner stone for the lockkeeper's house at the Three Mile Locks was laid near what is now the Boulevard Bridge, and by the turn of the century shallow packet boats or bateaux were carrying commodities and passengers around the falls from Shockoe to Westham. Eventually the canal company and its successor, the James River and Kanawha Canal Company, completed a 195-mile

Passengers watch from the roof of a canal boat as it nears Richmond.

system westward to Buchanan, Va. For nearly a century it was a vital link to the west.

The trip to Lynchburg took thirty-four and a half hours, while the return trip was one and a half hours shorter. The fare was $7.50 and included everything but drinks. George W. Bagby, a journalist, essayist, humorist and medical doctor wrote about his experiences on several trips, this one as a boy in the 1830's.

> At last we were off, slowly pushed along under the bridge on Seventh Street; then the horses were hitched; then slowly along till we passed the crowd of boats near the city, until at length with a lively jerk as the horses fell into a trot, away we went, the cut-water throwing up the spray as we rounded the Penitentiary hill, and the passengers lingered on the deck to get a last look at the fair City of Richmond, lighted by the pale rays of the setting sun.
>
> As the shadows deepened, everybody went below. There was always a crowd in those days, but it was a crowd for the most part of our best people, and no one minded it. I was little, and it took little room to accommodate me....
>
> Supper over, the men went on deck to smoke, while the ladies busied themselves with draughts or backgammon, with conversation or

with books. But not for long. The curtains which separated the female from the male compartment were soon drawn, in order that the steward and his aids might make ready the berths. These were three deep, "lower, middle, and upper," and great was the desire on the part of the men not to be consigned to the "Upper." Being light as cork, I rose naturally to the top, clambering thither by the leathern straps with the agility of a monkey, and enjoying as best I might the trampling overhead whenever we approached a lock…

The lamp shed a dim light over the sleepers, and all went well till some one — and there always was someone — began to snore…. "D--- that fellow! Chunk him in the ribs, somebody, and make him turn over. Is this thing to go on forever? Gentlemen, are you going to stand this all night? If you are, I am not. I am going to get up and dress. Who is he, anyhow? No gentleman would or could snore in that way!"

After a while silence would be restored, and all would drop off to sleep again, except the fellow in the upper berth, who, lying there, would listen to the *trahn-ahn-ahn-ahn* of the packet-horn, as we drew nigh the locks. How mournfully it sounded in the night....

We turned out early in the morning, and had precious little room for dressing.... The ceremony of ablution was performed in a primitive fashion. There were the tin basins, the big tin dipper and the long wooden handle. I feel it vibrating in the water now, and the water a little muddy generally; and there were the towels, a big one on a roller, and the little ones in a pile, and all of them wet. There were discomforts, it is true, but pshaw! one good, big, long, deep draught of pure, fresh morning air — one glimpse of the roseate flush above the wooded hills of the James, one look at the dew besprent bushes and vines along the canal bank — one sweet caress of dear mother nature in her morning robes, made compensation for them all....

For the men, this on-deck existence was especially delightful; it is such a comfort to spit plump into the water without the trouble of feeling around..., in the midst of a political discussion for the spittoon.

As for me, I often went below, to devour Dicken's earlier novels, which were then appearing in rapid succession. But, drawn by

Commodities carried on canal boats included cattle.

> the charm of the scenery, I would often drop my book and go back on deck again… [for] however bold and picturesque the cliffs and bluffs near Lynchburg and beyond, there was nothing from one end of the canal to the other to compare with the first sight [on the way back] of Richmond, when, rounding a corner not far from Hollywood, it burst full upon the vision, its capitol, its spires, its happy homes, flushed with the red glow of evening,….

At the time of Bagby's trip as a boy, there were 75 decked boats, 66 open boats, 54 bateaux and six passenger packets operating on the canal. During the peak year, 1860, the canal boats carried nearly a quarter million tons of tobacco, corn, lumber, iron ore, coal, stone, whisky, wheat, and other cargo. But with the development of trains in the late Nineteenth Century, rail transportation became faster and more economical than shipping via canal boats. Soon trains were traveling the canal towpath where mules pulled the canal boats a short time earlier.

Canal passengers would see this view today. On the opposite page is the view seen in the mid-1800's.

"Quarreling with the maggots"

RICHMOND'S Belle Isle, located in the middle of the James River, was the second worst confinement facility experienced by Union soldiers during the Civil War. Conditions — days with only watery "soup" to eat, tents for only about one-third of the prisoners to protect them from harsh weather — were so bad that Union soldiers were dying off at a rate of ten per day and up to 100 per day during winters. To get a feel for life in the prison, one needs only to turn to the diary of William Lee Goss, a member of the Second Massachusetts Heavy Artillery.

> I saw one day an Irish acquaintance who had possessed himself of bacon bone with some meat on it, but more maggots than Meat.

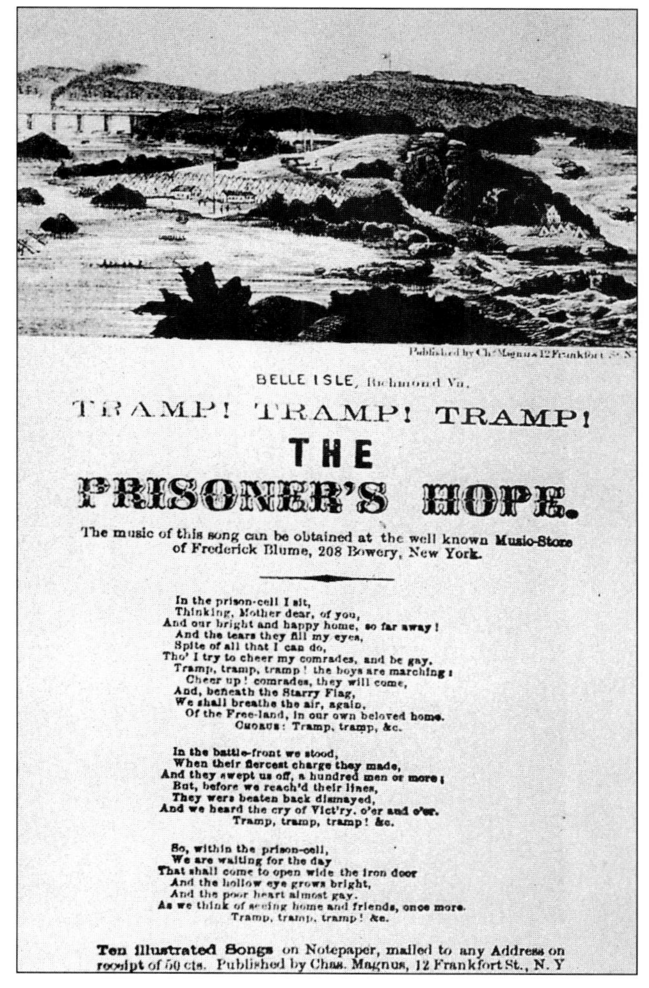

BELLE ISLE, Richmond Va.

TRAMP! TRAMP! TRAMP!

THE

PRISONER'S HOPE.

The music of this song can be obtained at the well known Music-Store of Frederick Blume, 208 Bowery, New York.

In the prison-cell I sit,
Thinking, Mother dear, of you,
And our bright and happy home, so far away!
And the tears they fill my eyes,
Spite of all that I can do,
Tho' I try to cheer my comrades, and be gay.
Tramp, tramp, tramp! the boys are marching;
Cheer up! comrades, they will come,
And, beneath the Starry Flag,
We shall breathe the air, again,
Of the Free-land, in our own beloved home.
CHORUS: Tramp, tramp, &c.

In the battle-front we stood,
When their fiercest charge they made,
And they swept us off, a hundred men or more;
But, before we reach'd their lines,
They were beaten back dismayed,
And we heard the cry of Vict'ry, o'er and o'er.
Tramp, tramp, tramp! &c.

So, within the prison-cell,
We are waiting for the day
That shall come to open wide the iron door
And the hollow eye grows bright,
And the poor heart almost gay,
As we think of seeing home and friends, once more.
Tramp, tramp, tramp! &c.

Ten illustrated Songs on Notepaper, mailed to any Address on receipt of 50 cts. Published by Chas. Magnus, 12 Frankfort St., N. Y

Belle Isle Prison was pictured on a Civil War song sheet.

> "What are you doing, Jim?" I interrogated.
>
> "Quarreling with the maggots," said Pat, with a comic leer, "to see who will have the bone,"
>
> Whereupon he brushed the maggots off, contemptuously, and went in for a meal.

More than 20,000 prisoners faced desperate conditions in the camp — by one account thousands died. One Union surgeon reported after a visit in the fall of 1863 that prisoners were dying off at a rate of ten per day and predicted the rate would rise that winter to one hundered per day. Another Union doctor reported in 1864 that 90 percent of the Union soldiers he examined there weighed less than 100 pounds.

Belle Isle Prison was established when the influx of Union prisoners became too great to be held in the city's other prisons — warehouses with the names of Ligon's, Mayo's, Taylors', Castle Thunder and Libby. Being in the center of the James River, it had the advantage of offering small chance of escape, for the river "at this point is very swift of current, and full of fantastic groups of rocks," noted Goss.

The prison was located on the eastern end of the island on a sandy area only a few feet above the water line. Drainage was poor, and made the location unhealthy. Overlooking the sandy area was a precipitous bluff, crowned with earthworks where the Confederates placed a cannon.

A Confederate cannon stood guard over Belle Isle Prison. The Richmond skyline is in the background.

Vermin were everywhere, reported Goss, in the prisoners' clothing, in their tents and in their food. A joke in the camp was that the vermin were so plentiful they held regimental drills in the mornings. But what was worse were the fleas, which "crawled over the ground from body to body," their attacks becoming more aggravated as the men became more emaciated. By daylight the fleas could be found and killed, and it gave the prisoners something to do. But at night the men had to suffer the bites.

"We hunted them three times a day but could not get the best of them," wrote Goss.

In the first year of the facility, the prisoners received adequate provisions, food and shelter. Typically each prisoner received a half pound of meat, potatoes, beans, rice, vinegar and salt daily, and was provided with tents for protection from the elements. But as the influx of prisoners increased during 1863, the costs of providing for them rose substantially.

In the summer of 1863 the prisoner exchange between the two enemies was suspended and the population of prisoners in the city multiplied, with nearly 6,000 being housed on Belle Isle. There were few tents and thousands of prisoners were forced to sleep on rocks or bare ground with no cover to protect them from the elements.

On a visit to the island during the fall of 1863, a Union inspector found 5,400 prisoners, many without "pants, shirts

Emaciated Union prisoners while away time on Belle Isle. Poor nourishment killed many.

or shoes" on half rations and without fuel or soap. By comparison Confederate prisoners held in some Northern camps were receiving meat three times a day, housing in wooden buildings and adequate clothing, official records show. (Thousands of Confederate prisoners, however, died at Northern prison facilities where conditions were nearly as bad as those at Belle Isle.)

Goss wrote:

> There were three stages of hunger in my experience; first, the common hungry craving one experiences after missing his dinner and supper; second, this passed away and was succeeded by a headache and a gnawing at the stomach; then came weakness, trembling of the limbs, which if not relieved by food, was followed by death."
>
> Ordinarily we received just enough food to keep us hungry… Men became, under such surroundings, indifferent to almost everything, except their own miseries….
>
> Near the… west side of the camp, were one or two wild cherry trees, which formed the only shade in the prison limits, and… their branches had been cut off for fuel in spite of the vigilance of the guard, and the necessity of shade for the prisoners. Here, one afternoon, I found a German dying. No one was there to care for him and soothe his dying

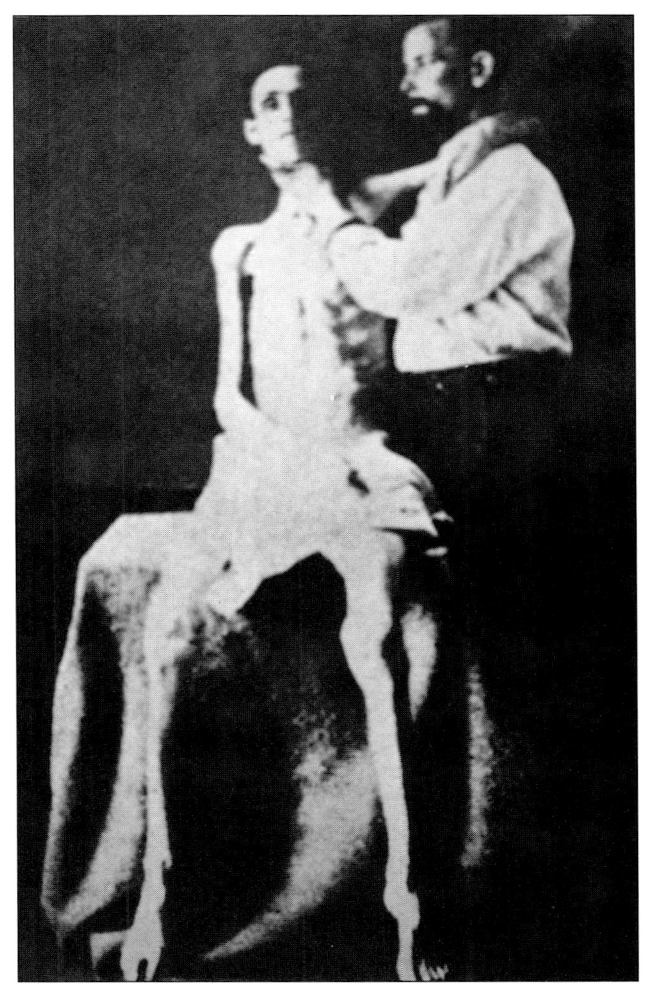

A Union doctor examines a soldier who was held on Richmond's Belle Isle.

> moments; the parched, filthy ground was his deathbed, over his wasted hands and sunken face the flies were gathering, while the disgusting sores of his flesh swarmed with maggots and other vermin. Moved by such a spectacle, I sat down by his side to brush the flies from his pallid face, and moisten the parched lips with the water from my canteen. Quite a number thereupon gathered around. One professing sympathy with so pitiable an object, suggested that he would feel better to have his boots off, and forth with pulling them off, coolly walked away with them and sold them. I afterwards met and recognized him, and expressed very freely my opinion that he had been guilty of a detestable act, unworthy of anything human. He confessed that it was rather rough, but excused himself by saying he was hungry, and thought it not so bad to steal from a dying man as from one likely to live; and he thought the boots would do him more good than a dead man.

The dead were put in wooden coffins and carried off the island the next day by the wagons that came over each morning with bread from the city bakeries. As conditions worsened, the number of coffins increased.

> Our rations at this time (1863) consisted of one half loaf to each man per day, and beans, cooked in water in which bacon had been

Graves of Union prisoners who died on Belle Isle. The bodies were later removed to other cemeteries.

> boiled for the guard, — usually containing about twenty per cent of maggots, — owing to scarcity of salt; thirty per cent, of beans and the remainder in water. There may have been a very small percentage of salt, but the fact was not ascertainable by the sense of taste.... It was issued sometimes twice a week, and sometimes not at all....

Reports from Richmond told of the overcrowding, poor conditions and death at Belle Isle and other Richmond prisons. President Abraham Lincoln approved a raid on Richmond to free the prisoners, but it failed. Confederate officials, however decided to move the prisoners to Andersonville, Georgia, the worst prison in the South.

Bizarre story

Union Colonel Killed Leading Attack on Richmond

BODY BURIED TWICE; THEN STOLEN

Woman Spy Suspected in Plot

THE above headlines might have appeared in the Richmond *Whig* in March 1864 if details of one of the strangest incidents to have occurred during the Civil War were known then as they are now, 129 years later. The story involved these factors — Union Colonel Ulric Dahlgren was killed during a raid on Richmond. His body was dumped in a shallow grave. A day later it was dug up, brough to Richmond and reburied below Oakwood Cemetery. The following night the body was stolen by Union sympathizers in a plot hatched by a woman who was suspected of spying for the Union Army. Then the body was reburied under three peach trees on a Henrico County farm.

Elizabeth Van Lew

The story begins with the woman, Elizabeth Van Lew, who lived in a magnificent mansion on Richmond's Church Hill. Raised in Richmond, she was educated in Philadelphia where she began formulating her abolitionist leanings. After her father, a prominent Richmond merchant, died in 1843, she convinced her mother to free the servants they owned. By the beginning of the Civil War she had purchased some of the relatives of the servants and had freed them also. When Virginia seceeded, Miss Van Lew, a bird-like looking woman, vowed to do whatever she could to help the Union defeat the South and to end slavery. She set up a spy network and soon was sending information on Confederate troop movements and conditions in Richmond to Union General Benjamin F. Butler, commander of the Army of the James.

Miss Van Lew often acquired her information by visiting Union officers held at the city's Libby Prison, taking them food on plates with false bottoms and books, in which the officers hid their notes. She also gathered information on conditions of prisoners at Belle Isle, where noncommissioned Union soldiers were held on the island in the middle of the James River.

By January 1864 the Richmond prisons were crowded with captured Union soldiers and conditions had deteriorated to a point that prisoners kept on Belle Isle were dying off at a rate of 100 or more a day, according to soldiers' diaries later published.

The pressure of feeding thousands of prisoners led Confederate officials to make plans to move many of them to Andersonville, Georgia, and Miss Van Lew sent this letter to General Butler January 30:

"It is intended to remove to Georgia very soon all the Federal prisoners; butchers and bakers to go at once. They are already notified and selected. Quaker [another Union spy in Richmond] knows this to be true."

She then suggested a raid be attempted on Richmond, to free the prisoners "with [no] less than 30,000 cavalry, [and] from 10,000 to 15,000 infantry to support them...."

General Butler marked her message "private and immediate," and forwarded it to Washington.

Whether the dispatch precipitated the actual raid that occurred a month later is debated by historians, but, nevertheless, a raid was attempted. On February 15, President Abraham Lincoln called in Brigadier General Judson

Kilpatrick to discuss the raid. At the end of the meeting the president gave his approval and two weeks later Kilpatrick and Colonel Dahlgren, twenty-two-year-old son of Admiral John A. Dahlgren, left Rapidan near Fredericksburg and headed south towards Richmond with 3,500 cavalrymen.

After a skirmish with Confederate soldiers near Taylorsville in New Kent County, February 29th, the force was split and Colonel Dahlgren took 500 men to approach Richmond from the west. As Dahlgren's men skirted the city's outer defenses, word reached Richmond of the impending raid. The alarm was sounded from the bell tower in Capitol Square and the local defense brigade, consisting of old men and boys, wounded veterans and factory workers under Brigadier General Custis Lee, R.E. Lee's son, rushed out to a point on Cary Street Road two miles west of the city's limits. There they blocked Dahlgren's raiders on March 2. Facing probable defeat that dark, wet night, Dahlgren ordered his men to retrace their route north and east around the city in an attempt to link up again with General Kilpatrick.

Confederates of Fitzhugh Lee's cavalry division under Captain E.C. Fox and Lieutenant James Pollard got ahead of Dahlgren's men and set up an ambush at Mantapike Hill between King and Queen Court House and King William Court House. Dahlgren was killed and over a hundred of his men captured.

His body was unceremoniously dumped in a shallow

grave. The little finger of his right hand was cut off for a souvenir, and his false, lower right leg was stolen. The next day his body was dug up and sent to Richmond, put on display, taunted by onlookers, and then secretly reburied below Oakwood Cemetery under cover of darkness. (Richmond's newspapers claimed that papers found on Dahlgren's body showed he planned to burn the city and kill President Jefferson Davis, and publication of the alleged papers inflamed citizens. Historians, however, dispute the existence of the papers.)

Learning of his death and where his body was now buried, Miss Van Lew arranged for friends to steal the body and bring it to a Henrico farmhouse, where she waited. In her secret journal she later wrote a strange, almost idolizing description of the corpse:

> Col. Dahlgren's hair was very short, but all that could be spared was cut off.... Gentle hands and tearful eyes examined his breast to see if there was any wound there, but nothing of the kind could be perceived. The body, except for the head was in a perfect state of preservation, fair, fine and firm the flesh.... The comeliness of the young face was gone, yet the features seemed regular and there was a wonderful look of firmness of energy stamped upon them.

Col. Ulric Dahlgren

After Miss Van Lew completed her examination, the body was put into a new coffin; loaded on a wagon; driven to the defense lines around Richmond; stopped at least once, but not searched because the Confederate sentry recognized the German farmer driver and waved him on after a friendly conversation, and buried for the third time on another farm under three peach trees.

Meanwhile Colonel Dahlgren's parents were frantic to have the body of their son brought home. Admiral Dahlgren pleaded with Lincoln to telegram Confederate President Davis asking for the body. This was done and Davis ordered the body disinterred from Oakwood Cemetery. Miss Van Lew, however, had intervened to Davis' great embarrassment.

Although she did send a lock of Dahlgren's hair to the family sometime later, it was not until after the war that the Admiral learned where the body was buried and recovered it. For her work as a spy, Ulysses S. Grant appointed Miss Van Lew postmistress of Richmond for the two terms he was President.

Thomas Jefferson's Capitol

As U.S. minister to France in 1785, former Virginia governor and author of the Declaration of Independence, Thomas Jefferson, fell in love. He gazed for hours at a time "like a lover at his mistress," he wrote. His passion was not for a woman, but a temple — the Roman temple at Nimes, France, that, in his words was "one of the most beautiful, if not the most beautiful and precious morsels of architecture left to us by antiquity."

The temple would become the model for Jefferson's Virginia Capitol building, which the General Assembly had authorized in 1780 to be built on Shockoe Hill in Richmond, a location that must have caused some Richmonders to question the assemblymen's wisdom. The area was cut deeply

The General Assembly first met in Richmond in this barn-like building at Fourteenth and Cary streets.

with gullies and ravines that had to be filled, and the square of land was bordered on the east by a country road that wound down a steep and dangerous hill.

While the plans for the building were being completed and actual construction done — the cornerstone was laid August 18, 1785 — the Assembly met in a two-story wooden, barn-like building at Fourteenth and Cary Streets. A German doctor visiting Richmond at the time, Johann David Schopf, described several scenes at this first Richmond "capitol" building.

> At the open door of the hall stands a doorkeeper, who is almost incessantly and with a loud voice calling out for one member after another. In the anteroom there is a tumult quite as constant; here they amuse themselves zealously with talk of horseraces, runaway negroes, yesterday's play, politics.... In the same clothes in which one goes hunting or tends his tobacco-fields, it is permissible to appear in the Senate or the Assembly. There are displayed boots, trousers, stockings, and Indian leggins, great-coats, ordinary coats, and short jackets, according to each man's caprice or comfort....

In October, 1788, the General Assembly began meeting in the new Capitol with its brick exterior and leaky roof. Samuel Mordecai, who published his memories of Richmond in 1856, described the conditions of the new Capitol.

Thomas Jefferson's Capitol as depicted in 1830 engraving.

> The *Capitol* itself, not then stuccoed, exposed its bare brick walls between the columns or pilasters. The roof was once flat, if I mistake not, and paved with tiles, and, like Noah's Ark, "was pitched without, with pitch." But as a hot sun caused the pitch to flow down the gutters, and the rains to enter the halls, an elevated roof was substituted.

Scotsman Isaac Weld, Jr., visiting the city as the Capitol was being completed, wrote that "from the opposite side of the river this building appears extremely well, but on close inspection it proves to be a clumsy, ill-shapen pile." But Duke de la Rochefoucauld-Liancourt of France found the building "beyond comparison, the finest, the most noble and the greatest in all America."

For many years the square below the Capitol was unfenced and the ground was covered with gravel and weeds on which cows and goats grazed. Finally in 1818 an iron fence was erected to enclose the grounds, but there was still the unsightly, dilapidated wooden barracks occupied by the Public Guard and their families, whose members did not hesitate to hang their washing out for all to see, including the distinguished members of the legislature. The barracks were replaced in 1824 by the brick bell tower.

During the Civil War the Capitol sustained damage more from neglect than from the war or the fire after the

Union soldiers stand in the Capitol grounds after Richmond fell April 3, 1865. The building in the foreground burned to the ground during the fire that day.

Confederate Government evacuated the city April 2. The occupying Union Army used the building as its headquarters and many Confederate soldiers reluctantly came to the House chambers to give their oath of allegiance to the Union. For the next five years, Virginia was run by a federally-appointed governor, Francis H. Pierpont and a legislature that included black representatives.

With the end of federal rule in 1870, an incident occurred that proved to be one of the city's greatest tragedies. The General Assembly gave Governor Gilbert C. Walker approval to appoint a new Richmond City Council. That body elected Henry D. Ellyson, publisher of the Richmond *Dispatch*, as its mayor. But the sitting mayor, George Chahoon of New York, refused to vacate this office. The Virginia Supreme Court of Appeals was called upon to settle the matter, and a hearing was held in the courtroom on the third floor of the Capitol. Hundreds of people crowded into every foot of space in the room and its gallery April 27, 1870.

A report the next day in the Richmond *Whig* told what happened:

> At 11 o'clock... a crack was heard as if a gun had been exploded beneath the Body! All eyes turned towards the centre floor under the gallery, from whence the sound proceeded.... Again the sound was heard, and immediately to the horror of all present, the floor began to give

Rescuers work to free dead and injured after courtroom floor collapsed.

> way and began to fall to the floor below with a fearful crash, followed by not only the gallery and its weight of humanity, but by the timbers overhead, by which the courtroom was attached.... A wail of horror immediately followed by the shrieks of suffering mortals....

Two judges, W.T. Joynes and F.T. Anderson were in the courtroom awaiting their colleagues. They were able to scamper to the conference room, but most of the others in the courtroom fell forty feet to the House of Delegates below. Many were crushed to death and others suffocated. The dead and injured were covered with blood and dust. They were carried to the Capitol lawn where many were unrecognizable until the blood and dust were cleaned from their faces.

Sixty-two men, including Patrick Henry Aylett, grandson of Patrick Henry and prominent attorney and journalist, J.W.D. Bland, a black senator from Prince Edward County; John Turner, a member of the House from Page County; and Henry County Mayor Samuel Hairston were among those who died.

Among the 251 injured were the rival mayors and ex-Governor H.H. Wells.

The Capitol was remodeled and two wings and granite steps to the portico were added between 1904 and 1906. Another renovation was done between 1962 and 1964, but did not change the exterior of the building.

Re-enactors hold ceremony beside Houdin's statue of George Washington during reburial of Confederate soldiers.

"Both men fired…"

JUST three years after the collapse of the Capitol courtroom came another tragedy. The sky was still overcast May 9, 1873, from a storm that had drenched the state the two previous days, as the two young men stood facing each other in the early evening. Each, one bearded and the other sporting a mustache, stood with loaded Colt Navy pistols in a field near the Oakwood Cemetery. Both men had served in the Confederate Army and were calm as they looked into one another's gun barrel.

One of the seconds later reported:

> We placed the men; the word was given; both men fired; and both missed. Tabb said to McCarty, "Are you satisfied?" McCarty replied: "Oh, no. I demand another fire…." Again the word was given; both men fired and both fell.

Mary Triplett was one of Richmond's most beautiful belles during the 1800's.

The duel revolved around one of Richmond's most beautiful belles, Mary Triplett, 23, who was noted for her regal carriage and her long, blond curling hair. She was described by one of her contemporaries as a "veritable daughter of the Gods, divinely fair and most divinely tall… with wondrous expressive eyes."

Page McCarty, a journalist and unsuccessful suitor of Miss Triplett, was described as "an attractive devil-may-care sort of fellow."

John B. Mordecai, a nephew of Samuel Mordecai, author of "*Richmond In Bygone Days,*" was one of Miss Triplett's latest suitors, and completely in love.

During the Richmond German, the society dance of the year, a friend of McCarty maneuvered Mary through the first of the figures so that she ended up facing McCarty. Mary danced a few steps with her former suitor and then walked off the floor.

The next morning there appeared a verse in the Richmond *Enquirer.*

> The First Figure in the German When Mary's queenly form I press, in Strauss's latest waltz/ I would as well her lips caress, although those lips be false./ For still with fire love tips his darts, and kindles up anew./The flame which once consumed my heart, when those dear lips were true./ Of form so fair, or faith so faint, if

truth were only in her./ Though she'd be the sweetest saint, I'd still feel like a sinner.

Though the poetry was not signed, Mordecai had no doubt of its author and when the two later met in a bar of the Richmond Club, heated words were exchanged. A fight broke out; the two were separated by friends, but settlement on the "field of honor" was never in doubt.

McCarty

Both men were wounded and Mordecai died a few days later. William Royall, a friend of Mordecai, recorded that "an hour before his ending… [Mordecai] sent for me. Putting his arms around my neck he pulled my ear down to his mouth and whispered, 'Remember, Royall, what I told you.' I answered, "I certainly shall, John.' It was a message to his sweetheart."

Mordecai

McCarty was fined $500 and sentenced to six months in jail, suspended on a doctor's certificate stating that his health would be endangered. He recovered. Mary Triplett married Phillip Haxall, one of Mordecai's friends.

Monument Avenue

IN May, 1890 thousands of Richmonders and admirers from across the country gathered in a field west of the city at what is now Allen Avenue to watch the unveiling of Antonin Mercie's statue of Robert E. Lee, the commander of the Army of Northern Virginia during the Civil War.

For thirteen years the statue stood alone before the first house was built on what would become one of the most beautiful and famous byways in the United States, Monument Avenue.

The avenue is an outdoor art museum of statues and 20th Century houses, and has a broad, green ribbon of trees and grass where people jog, walk their dogs or throw Frisbees.

Monument Avenue had its beginning when it was decided there should be a statue to Lee. John Allen owned land between Broad Street and Park Avenue, west of the city limits

Workmen assemble Lee Monument.

and his offer of a site on which to place the monument was accepted. The statue arrived at Main Street train station May 7, 1890. Citizens assembled that afternoon to pull the cargo, which filled four boxcars, to the Allen tract. The task turned into a festive parade. The ropes used to pull the stone base and bronze sculpture of Lee sitting on his horse, Traveller, were cut into pieces and given to those who participated. The statue was unveiled May 29, 1890, before 25,000 people.

Development of the avenue was delayed, however, because of a poor economy. The first house was built at what is now the 2000 address, and the street was officially named Monument Avenue in 1906. Soon the avenue became the place to live. Nationally known architects designed and built huge houses there; some contained elevators and servants' quarters. Using stone and brick walls 18-inches thick, the architects designed them to last and most of the original structures exist today.

"Every architect and designer was trying to show how good he could do a house or a building," Richmond architect Robert Winthrop told the *Richmond News Leader* in an interview.

About a fifth of the first families to buy or build houses there were immigrants or first generation Americans, according to the 1910 Census. The 1903 city land book indicates that the first group of houses were built on the north side of the 1600 block by W. J. Payne. The largest home on the avenue is the Branch House at Davis and

The Lee Monument today.

Monument. It contains 24,000 square feet and was built by John Russell Pope. Many native Richmonders refer to it as "the castle."

In 1915 the avenue was extended into Henrico County, but it is the portion of the avenue within the city limits along which the houses are the most elegant and distinctive. Many of these houses are still privately owned, but others were converted to apartment buildings.

Along with the Lee statue, four other statues honor Confederates — J.E.B. Stuart, Jefferson Davis, Thomas J. "Stonewall" Jackson and Matthew Fontaine Maury.

When dignitaries arrived in Richmond by train at the Broad Street Station, they were driven down to City Hall or to the Governor's Mansion along Monument Avenue. These notables included Winston Churchill, Gen. Dwight D. Eisenhower, Charles A. Lindbergh, and two World War I heroes — British Prime Minister David Lloyd George and French Marshal Ferdinand Foch, commander of the Allied forces.

Now thousands of Richmond area residents promenade down the avenue on Easter Sunday. The event is one of the highlights of the year for people of all social and economic strata.

Thousands of people attend the annual Easter Parade held on Monument Avenue, shown above and on the opposite page.

The roof gave way...

THOMAS J. Mason, an engineer for the Chesapeake & Ohio Railway, eased the work train about 100 feet into the tunnel at North Nineteenth Street at the base of Jefferson Park. A work force of several hundred was rehabilitating the 52-year-old tunnel that ran under Church Hill.

Lemy Campbell, a black laborer, was working near the west entrance shortly after 3 p.m., October 2, 1925. Suddenly he heard the sound of bricks falling from the tunnel roof. Several more fell as he looked up. Campbell dropped his tools and ran for the entrance, the screams of other workers ringing in his ears.

Mason looked up just as the bricks, earth and timber came smashing down, tearing loose electrical wires and throwing the tunnel into blackness. Mason was pinned to his seat by the reverse lever. His fireman, B.F. Mosby, jumped out of the cab and began crawling underneath the tender. The

Rescuers constructed a shaft to reached the buried train.

crush of the cave-in cracked the engine's boiler and scalding steam blew over him. Screaming from the pain, he dragged his body along under the ten flatcars towards the eastern exit 4,000 feet away. Most of the other workers were also picking their way towards that direction, feeling in the darkness along the wet walls. Mosby's screams were heard by fleeing workers and several ran back and pulled him from under the flatcars. In what only took minutes, but seemed an eternity, the workers reached the end of the tunnel.

As he was loaded in an ambulance, Mosby pleaded with the others who escaped to contact his wife and baby girl, and tell them he escaped and that he was not badly hurt. But the burns proved fatal and he died that night in the hospital.

Conductor C.G. McFadden was standing between two flat cars near the engine when the roof fell, knocking him to the ground and breaking his shoulder. He too crawled under the flatcars and was helped out of the tunnel by Brakeman C.S. Kelso.

Brakeman A.G. Adams was knocked to the ground and stunned for a few moments. But he too was able to grope his way through the darkness by crawling under the flatcars to safety.

The roof continued to crumble and quickly the engine, and Mason, dead or alive, were cut off from rescue.

By nightfall a steam shovel had begun to dig a shaft from Jefferson Park, directly above the train tunnel. Rescue parties were digging from each end of the tunnel towards Mason. Huge crowds of onlookers swarmed to the scene.

C&O officials called the roll of laborers and announced that only two other men besides Mason were missing, R. Lewis and H. Smith, but the workers were skeptical, insisting 10 to 15 men were still in the tunnel.

After nine days of arduous digging, a worker cut his way through the floor of a flatcar and crawled underneath to the engine. The light from his lantern showed the decomposed body of Mason sitting upright in the cab. Further searchers failed to find any more bodies, but hundreds of tons of earth still covered the area between the engine and the western entrance of the tunnel.

Because of the danger of further cave-in, the tunnel is sealed at both ends. Are the crushed bones of black laborers R. Lewis and H. Smith buried there? What of the others the workers insisted were missing?

Ironically the tunnel had been out of use for 24 years when the cave-in occurred. It had become obsolete when the C&O completed its steel viaduct along the river from Fulton in 1901. The workers were in the tunnel to reopen and enlarge it for use again.

Train tunnel

First woman bank president

As Richmond entered the 20th Century, a woman stepped forth and began to make a quiet and unusual impact on the community. Soon she would become the first woman bank president in the country. But what was more remarkable was that she was an African-American woman in a city dominated by white male politicians and businessmen.

She was Maggie L. Walker.

A tall, large woman with clear kindly eyes and a firm mouth, Mrs. Walker was born in 1867 to a mother who, soon widowed, was forced to live in an alley and take in washing to make enough money to feed her children. Maggie Lena

Maggie L. Walker, right, with members of her staff.

Mitchell worked alongside her mother until she graduated from high school. After teaching for several years, she joined the Independent Order of St. Luke in 1889 as executive secretary, receiving $8 a month. The Order was similar to others like it in the black community where members paid small weekly dues that were used to help them in later life when they became ill and to pay for their funeral expenses. There being no black banks, nor any white banks providing savings accounts for would-be black customers, the orders filled the gap.

Miss Mitchell married Armstead Walker and continued to move up the ranks at the Order, becoming secretary-treasurer in 1899. She argued at work that if the Order could serve a thousand persons, why not ten thousand, a hundred thousand? With the energy of a dozen women, she took charge and by 1924 the organization had 100,000 members, a $100,000 building, a newspaper and employed fifty-five clerks in the home office here. There were 145 field workers and 15,000 children enrolled in the thrift clubs. Most importantly the organization had a bank, the St. Luke Penny Savings Bank & Trust Company — the oldest bank operated by blacks in the country. Mrs. Walker was its first president.

With the bank, blacks were able for the first time to save enough money on which to borrow to purchase a home or start a business. Noted Mrs. Walker in 1924:

...there was that one legged bootblack at Second and Cary Streets. He joined our Order. He had a rented chair out on the sidewalk in the weather. We helped him save, and when he had fifty dollars, we helped him rent a little place with three chairs.

That was seven years ago. Now he has a place of his own with twelve chairs. He has bought a home for his mother — paid $1,900 for it — and has it furnished and free of debt. And his bank account never falls below five hundred dollars.... Six hundred and forty-five homes have been paid for through our bank's help.

Numbers of our children have bank accounts from one hundred to four hundred dollars. They sell papers, cut grass, do chores, run errands, work in stores Saturday. We teach them the value of money....

Maggie Walker Museum

Despite the death of her husband, who was shot mistakenly by their son who thought his father was a burglar, and a fall that left her nearly paralyzed, she continued her work until her death in 1934.

The woman vanished

ON a hot August day in the 1890's, Governor Philip McKinney walked into his bedroom in the Governor's Mansion, and discovered a "striking young woman dressed richly in a taffeta evening gown" sitting at one of the room's windows. Her "beautiful smile" was "illuminated by the sunlight streaming through the window…," he later reported. So as not to embarrass her, he stepped quietly into his wife's room. Returning to his room a few minutes later, he found the woman had vanished.

The governor reported the incident, but no one could identify whom he had seen, nor shed any light on why she was there. She would reappear again and again for years to come. A Capitol policeman later reported seeing a woman standing in an upstairs bedroom where no unauthorized visitors were allowed. When he approached her, she disappeared before his eyes, leaving only fluttering curtains. Others have reported

One of Virginia's most famous ghosts, a woman, haunts the Governor's Mansion.

hearing footsteps and slamming doors in the mansion and one officer was in the basement when he "distinctly" felt something touch his face. He was so terrified that he quit his job.

Between 1970-1974, Governor Linwood Holton and his family occupied the mansion and the governor reported seeing a woman on the back stairs. She suddenly disappeared. When Tropical Storm Agnes swept through Richmond in 1972, a power failure cast the city into darkness. Still, a single bulb of a three-bulb fixture in the same stairway where Governor Holton had first seen the woman, kept burning. His wife, "Jinks," went to the Capitol and brought back with her Ann Compton, correspondent for a Roanoke television station, to witness the strange light. It was still burning and continued to do so even as Miss Compton, now White House correspondent for ABC News, and the Holtons tried every light switch to affect it.

On another occasion the Holtons found the salt shakers had been emptied all over the dining room table.

"She was a great tease. I suspect she's still [in the mansion]" Holton told a Richmond reporter in 1992. Asked why he and McKinney have been the only governors to report seeing the ghost, Holton said: "It may be that with ghosts, if you don't believe, then you don't see. But we believed, and we saw."

Ever since the courtroom floor collapsed in 1870 at the Capitol, killing 62, sounds have been heard in the night coming from the old House of Delegates chambers. Some say the sounds are only the normal creaks, groans and wind whistles of an old building, but others swear there are voices — soft, muted voices sobbing and moaning in the darkness.

In Richmond's northside neighborhood of Ginter Park stands "Westwood," a rambling old house used by Union Theological Seminary to house the families of married students. Originally the country home of Dr. Hunter Holmes McGuire, it was built in the nineteenth century. In 1942 this story was printed in the *Reader's Digest*:

> My mother went with my sister to live in Richmond, Virginia while my brother was studying there for the ministry. They rented a large, rambling old house. During the two years of her residence in this house, there frequently appeared before my mother an officer of the Confederate Army whose left sleeve had a band of [black] crape on it. She told my brother and sister of seeing the figure, but they teased her about. Later she told me, because I was a more sympathetic listener. She said that one day, tiring of his repeated appearances, she remarked to him as if he were human, "Oh why do you bother me so? I wish you would go away and leave me alone."

> He looked at her, sadly shook his head, vanished out of the diniing-room door, and never returned.
>
> Several months later, in some museum or art gallery, my sister was looking over the catalogue. Suddenly she said to my mother, "Here is a picture of your ghost." My mother's description of the apparition had been so accurate that my sister had recognized it immediately; and there, too, on the left sleeve was a band of [black] crape. The catalogue said the soldier in the picture was Dr. Hunter Holmes McGuire.

Dr. McGuire had been the personal physican of General "Stonewall" Jackson. One of the most famous and loved generals of the South during the Civil War, Jackson was struck mistakenly by bullets fired by his own men during the Battle of Chancellorsville in 1863. The general died several days later and Dr. McGuire wore a black crape on his arm in memory of his general.

Other Richmond ghosts have been reported at Hollywood Cemetery adjacent to Oregon Hill, and at the State Penitentiary on Belvidere Street until it was torn down in 1992. At the Ellen Glasgow House on East Main Street at Foushee, sounds of someone typing have been heard at night at the Nineteenth Century author's home.

Dr. Hunter Holmes McGuire

Christmas at Maymont Park, Nineteenth Century home of James H. Dooley.

Turkey and oysters were among the fresh food offered by a restaurateur on Main Street in the early 1900's.

Old City Hall reflected.

New City Hall reflected.

The Old Broad Street Railroad Station. It now houses the Science Museum of Virginia and the Ethyl Theater.

Two eras contrast in this 1981 picture of a steam engine pulling a train past Richmond's skyline buildings.

Recommended Reading

A Soldier's Story of His Captivity at Andersonville, Belle Isle, and Other Rebel Prisons. Warren Lee Goss. Boston: Richardson Co., 1871.

Chesterfield, An Old Virginia County. Francis Earl Lutz. Richmond: William Byrd Press, Inc., 1954.

Church Hill. The St. John's Church Historic District. Marguerite Crumley and John G. Zimmer. Richmond: Historic Richmond Foundation, 1991.

Fifty Years in Richmond, 1898-1948. Richmond: Valentine Museum, 1948.

Four Days in 1865. The Fall of Richmond. David D. Ryan. Richmond: Cadmus Communications Corporation, 1993.

General Lee's City. Richard M. Lee. McLean: EPM Publications Inc., 1987.

History of the James River & Kanawha Co. Wayland F. Dunaway. New York: AMS Press, 1969.

Lewis Ginter's Richmond. David D. Ryan. Richmond: Whittet & Shepperson, 1991.

Old Richmond Neighborhoods. Mary Wingfield Scott. Richmond: Whittet & Shepperson, 1950.

Richmond in By-Gone Days. Samuel Mordecai. Richmond: The Dietz Press, Incorporated, 1946 (reprint).

Recommended Reading (continued)

Richmond in Old Prints, 1737-1887. Alexander W. Weddell. Forword by Douglas S. Freeman. Richmond; Johnson Pub. Co., 1932.

Richmond-Her Past and Present. W. Asbury Christian. Richmond: L.H. Jenkins, 1912.

Richmond. The Story of A city. Virginius Dabney. Charlottesville: The University Press of Virginia, 1989 (revised and expanded edition).

The Capitol of Virginia. A Landmark of American Architecture. Fiske Kimball. Richmond: Virginia State Library and Archives, 1989.

The Falls of the James. David D. Ryan. Richmond: William Byrd Press, Inc., 1975.

The Ghosts of Richmond. L.B. Taylor, Jr. Williamsburg, 1985.

The History of Henrico County. Louis H. Manarin and Clifford Dowdy. Charlottesville: The University Press of Virginia, 1984.

The Secret Diary of William Byrd of Westover. Louis B. Wright and Marion Tinling. Richmond: William Byrd Press, Inc., 1941.

David D. Ryan is the author of six books on Virginia history, including *Four Days in 1865, The Fall of Richmond, Lewis Ginter's RICHMOND* and *The Falls of the James.*

Picture Credits

David D. Ryan: Front and back covers and pages 9, 11, 13, 27, 35, 61, 69, 70, 71, 79, 81, 88, 89, 90 and 91.

Edgar Allan Poe Museum: page 19.

Harpers Weekly: page 47.

Library of Congress: pages 39, 41, 43, 45, 57 and 59.

Maryland Historical Society: page 8.

Photographic History of the Civil War: page 51.

Richmond Newspapers, Inc.: pages 73 and 75.

Valentine Museum: pages 25, 63, 65, 77 and 86.

Virginia State Library and Archives: pages 10, 12, 15, 17, 23, 29, 33, 34, 37, 53 and 65.